Naked Testimonies

Naked Testimonies

Toyin Adewale-Gabriel

MALLORY PUBLISHING

Published by
Mallory Publishing,
Aylesbeare Common Business Park,
Exmouth Road,
Aylesbeare,
Devon,
EX5 2DG,
England

For a complete list of titles, visit
http://www.mallorypublishing.co.uk
e-mail: admin@mallorypublishing.co.uk

First published in this form 2006
by Mallory Publishing
Copyright © Toyin Adewale-Gabriel 1995,
1997, 2006

*First published in 1995. Second edition published in 1997
by Mace Associates, Lagos, Nigeria, ISBN 978 32456 2 7*

ISBN 1 85657 107 6

Cover design © Mallory International Limited
2006

All rights reserved. No part of this publication may be reproduced, stored in a retrieval system, or transmitted in any form or by any means, electronic, mechanical, photocopying, recording or otherwise, without the prior permission of the publishers.

Mallory Classic African Writing
An Introduction to the Series

Mallory International is one of the leading exporting booksellers in the United Kingdom, and works particularly in Africa, where our customers include many Ministries of Education, Universities, and other institutions.

We have found from experience that many classic works by African writers are out of print, or no longer available, and this series is intended to remedy that situation, making available for ongoing distribution a range of titles, both fiction and non-fiction, which might otherwise disappear.

I hope you enjoy this book. If you do, and you are aware of another important title which could usefully be reprinted, please contact us. E-mail addresses and contact details can be found on our web site.

Julian Hardinge,
Chairman,
Mallory International

CONTENTS

ACKNOWLEDGEMENTS 9

FOR T. J.	13
RECOMPENSE	14
ODIA	15
SALUTING LEONIE MCSWEENY	16
ARRIVALS	21
THE BRICK DISSOLVES IN THE CRYSTAL SEA	22
WAVES	23
BROKEN DAMS	24
AFTER SONG	25
INDEX	26
QUESTING	31
A POSTER	32
RUTH	33
THE LAST TEEN	34
SOUL-KIN	35
LEMON CREAM	36
HAIKU	37
RED FOR MEN	38
WATER COLOUR	39
AN EMBRACE	43
HER THREE DAYS	44
EVENING CHORUS	45
SOLITAIRE	46
TRIAL	47
IMPACT	49
A REJOICING	50
YOU SAY YOUR MOUTH HAS NO BLOOD	55

A THAWING	56
STREAMS I	57
STREAMS II	58
STREAMS III	59
AN EYE IS TALKING	60
MORNING	60
EVENING	61
NIGHT	62
DAY	63
NAKED TESTIMONIES 1	64
NAKED TESTIMONIES II	65
NAKED TESTIMONIES III	66
NAKED TESTIMONIES IV	67
NAKED TESTIMONIES V	68
LADEN	73
RAIN	74
SIDEWALK LULLABY	75
YOU CANNOT AVOID ME	76
UNTITLED	77
FRESH DAWNS	78

ACKNOWLEDGEMENTS

On this morning of rejoicing I exalt the Word who became flesh for the World.
Many of the poems appearing in this collection have been previously published in the following anthologies, journals and newspapers:
Twenty Nigerian Writers
The Literary Review, (Fairleigh Dickinson University)
Okike
For Ken For Nigeria
ANA Review
Ase, Anthology of the National Library of Poetry U.S.A. (1995)
...und auf den strafsen eine Pest.
The Guardian
The Daily Times
The Punch
The Concord
The Post Express Literary Supplement
The Statesman
The Tribune.

Some have also been presented on the Television Programme, *Arts Alive* by Mr. Ben Tomoloju.

Toyin Adewale - Gabriel
Lagos
March, 1997.

Regards...

FOR T. J.

(After viewing the film, *The Champ*)

If this were the grave separation
how many flowers would I plant
to spell forget-me-not?
Strangely, I sense darkness is soon to occur.

And beyond this prison
I am a frozen ice-cream
stubbornly awaiting you in the immense stadium
where love is sparkling like face cleanser
and fire,
passionate, consuming, melting the epiphanies of grief.

Our warm tears are museums
of faithfulness, of chocolates, my quick forgiveness
when you steal my only coin
They are ancestors of a gift so suicidal
only blood will ribbon it
on the night you will become Santa Claus
bearing me a pricey present
in the boxing arena.

It will be a night of star spangles
that shall become tear drenched
A night when I shall not attain
the joy after which I grope
O, champ, you will sleep too finally
my fear will come true, it will become
a tattoo prick drilling deep in my flesh
I will waaaiiillll
and across the cinema rows
my plea will slap a poet
and then, you and I shall take flesh in word.

RECOMPENSE

(For Vincent Van Gogh)

Your gravestone full of teeth
broods over the potato eaters
O lover of sien!
The ivy is singing, blooming
bearing seed for a hundred years
life has poured time into you,
poured a zillion dollars bombed to ash
And the wretched still mystify
raining yellows, vibrant red and glorious
green on canvases
but ears stick on now....
I hear Handel's sonata
as the flame fries your hand, your books
grilling your heart.
Detained by the tongues of men
the sea arrives too late
Already you're a hot dog loved by too many
Yet from the chicken coop, they march out
Your canvases: they hold their catastrophes,
their calm.

ODIA

Dashing antelope
turbulence of warring waters
bottled together
ocean wave, ever ocean wave
whirlwind,
now off!

SALUTING LEONIE MCSWEENY

Alone and stumbling
whose heart tarries in vain
when virgin road signs
are composed in the famine of rainbows

Heed the singing voice

My heart is crippled
lead me to the Rock
that is higher than I

Blow, song, blow where you will
Tease the dark
Dare, song, laugh where you will.

Train...

ARRIVALS

Night of bread, night of vows
starbright night, lighthouse night!

All night I walk with you on twin roads
in a shower of silver confetti
the trumpet hastens us to the crossroads
hear the plaintive horns
in the pipes of my open wound
you and I and the yawning miles
under the pawpaw tree
we have signed the thunder drums
if the moon now declaims our names
if stars gossip about farewells
I know you will fly home alive
the cacti will become fecund paste.

THE BRICK DISSOLVES IN THE CRYSTAL SEA

(for Sesan Ajayi)

The brick dissolves in the crystal sea
The hour of life has come
Take your bow
Voice of a horn, of flutes, of drums and cymbals
Stride the ancient orchestra

You have inherited the word
Its flesh, its wine
It is bread, it is blood
What fire in our bones
Sad rivers, the infinite ache...

The night is afflicted with arrows
The wind your companion is whispering
Greet the throne of sapphire with the
Voice of centuries...
You stroke a note rich in sun and song.

WAVES

Because your waves
spur my breaststrokes

Because you are the lowest common
denominator
infinite and endless

Because you tumble in silence, rumble like an
earthquake
Because you are a whisper, a loud urging voice.

A sober grey, a love blue, of wind and cloven
fires
Bold and verdant

I swim, coasting on your chest
In your bowels, lies my rare life, O Spirit! Endfold
it, root me in your sensory nerves that I when I
awake shall be certified
free and bound.

BROKEN DAMS

See the quarrel of waters, the
helpless peace of the sea at its wits end
see, this flapping red flag
is a pathological liar
the pine trees, sentries beyond are truth

See, nautical miles
of silver swims bereft of crab bites
refreshing as spring water from
earth's bowels

I set you a ruby
with amethysts and clouds

I break free perfume
from the house of laughter
I dismantle the belts, my dams
at your table, O delectable soup
fill me up!
Delightful, delightful are you on my budsl

AFTER SONG

Today, I roar like a lion
hungry to prowl
the yawning kilometres of dawn
but steel clangs in
bars me, binds me, unbinds me

You are the restraint,
the crucial divorce from desert paths
the narrow path that
urgently demands my presence
You are the challenge that won't let me grieve
Today, you are a cage, my great freedom.

INDEX

(for Kunle Ajibade)

The entries of your eyes
are the catalogues of a library
Hassled. Squinting. Questioning
Like metal detectors
Rags. Rain.
Red is the index that pain is...

Vistas...

QUESTING

How does it feel
when your nests are ants, soldier ants,
when creative concepts
relish the welcome rug?
When response is indifferent
to the stimuli of flesh.
How is jellyfish on strange sand?
The third-rate adverts of rival wives,
barren calm, spurn steel
damning decrees, severing sods?
Tell me, what is the sound of breaking terracotta?

A POSTER

Within you
verdant hills tease a thunderous waterfall
beneath a potent sky
A sun, the shade of mischief
pours a warm morning on steep mountain paths
Dare I climb to the heady songs of
a thousand different birds, a different thousand
leaves
to hug words of peace
whose tips root soul deep
at the querulous waters
where there is full fruit

RUTH

What return is there
when the ten-stringed lyre invites me
to the harvest of new barley
in the fields of the All-Sufficient One
I shall cross the Jordan and humble
the harsh Judean sun with a flick of my blue shawl
I will challenge our solitary acre to a duel
and wrestle from it an amazing grace
so Naomi, intreat me not to depart from you
nor to refrain from wearing my dancing sandals
and my labourer's arms

I come to glean in your farms, Bethlehem
I spurn nothing, I thresh trampled grain
that Naomi and I might live life
but there's a raging cold inside me
who shall extend the border of
his garment over me?
Naomi says yours is the joy O Boaz
she bids me wear perfume and lace
she pours kerosene on my widow's weeds
How lively were the lanes the night
I strolled to the threshing floor
the moon was fluorescence to my feet,
winds attended me, invading
Boaz with my scent. He stirred,
and woke. And windows were put into blank walls
doors where there were no entries
my rough roads became a dual carriageway
a fore-runner of the Christ,
leading from Moab to Israel, from men to God
and Naomi, I have fought well by your side
and earned a new meaning for my name;
I am better than seven sons.

THE LAST TEEN

Sorting out bits of cards and desires
time strides in like a sober invigilator
lugging a deciding quiz
filing cabinets arise within me
a ticking clock, a horn, a clarion call

Here the spades shall be called spades
and themes by their right tags
on honest slabs where
my spirit shall lay pruned
in the clinical wards of forever
How shall I score in the hour-glass
before this jury of witnesses?
What art shall install what honour in what hall?

Here lies a poet who shopped in
trivia street and stored in transistory avenue
She took vacations at crisisville and
worshipped at damnhollow where the
notion of a Lord God is an unspeakable
abomination.

And alive here is a thermal river
springing impactful currents
a joy song against the
bleak deserts that rattle minted mornings.

SOUL-KIN

The delightful has befallen me
for your belly-deep laughter
possess these hours of vibrant poetry
hours of nurturing lilacs
excavating the essence of history
on a beach front.

I am arrested by breezy bike rides
in the war-red sun
I am awed by the truth
of plants grown up in their youth
I write, exhilarated by the sloshing freedom;
the resounding dams of the rainbow spirit.

Beneath brilliant nights
tenderness becomes the jack plane of
rough diamonds
the rhythm of an eternal gospel
in your stride, in the star light.

LEMON CREAM

Like never before, we conquer our stammering

Phrases no longer trail away
No, we catch them and instil in them
the speech of open, confident rhythm

Bubbles arise within you
laden with coconut flavour
and your laughter as forceful as
rushing waters heads to wash me clean
in the meeting hall of our openness

Soon, thereafter, peace will step in to our door
to an embrace possessed of silence
and we will merge, I the lemon, you the cream.
We shall be christened Lemon Cream
I ripen, ready and reaching.

HAIKU

It's your brass shield
They are your streaks of sun
This silence... these slammed gates.

RED FOR MEN

(for G...)

The wind pours laughter and four-letter words
dreams spill in this hot house of popping corn
over piles of fried yam and breweries, the calabash
is replete with mischief and castrated greek gods...

He would light the moon with fire
He would tickle the viper in a play bath
He is red in the bullring
He is a wave on the seashore

Cliff-hanger, squaring the noon sun
Bird to fire
He is searching the wind for songs...
May the wind blow where he will.

WATER COLOUR

Sea sees sky
The sand brims with ivory
Azure tumbles
The water is sterling silver in a tumbler

At night
Where is blue
and ivory
and tumbling azure?

Expressions...

AN EMBRACE

Welcome
the moon when it is full blown
know its glowing dance
indulge, regally

Welcome
silence before guarara falls,
your miraculous life
Kneel, kneel and be still

Welcome
calm in the blasting wind
shake the shawls
nurture the coral bed

Welcome
the swollen ragged edge of bananas
drink from the upper and lower springs
It is sowing time, it is reaping time.

Welcome the gentle whisper after the earth quakes.

HER THREE DAYS

Let the camwood rejoice
flow O perfumed river
flood me like driving rain

Let my hut wear the pride of a palace
let mosquitoes lose their teeth
for three nights of ivory and beads

Luxuriant black soap,
spare not, know me in imperial lather
before the caress of coconut oil

Let kitchen themes be a
kings portion for the dashing stag
on the mountains of my desire

Come my three days
with the seven winds
over four green lights, proceed.

No? Not? Never?

Lost in the loins of a new enticement
you despise my three days
your disdain is a flaring match stick

Igniting thorns beneath my spurned arms your
lance pierces my soul
with a familiar wail-song

What is man that I'm mindful of him?

EVENING CHORUS

Sparkling is the earth now
from rain's facial scrub
sparkling like you from your evening shower
A wet breeze conjures you in
images of wind, poetry and jeans.

You are as wind, tender respite on a
sweltering night, warm upon my nerve ends
you are the late and early rains
bearing seed to the sower and sweet oranges
You are poetry, you are sometimes jeans
You are the wind dance
the deluge of rain in desert places
my spontaneous poet!
Primed jeans for a morning walk
The breeze teases now, wafts you
like a delicious aroma
And I know a rearing towards you
my soul rumbles hungrily for you.

SOLITAIRE

On Valentine's Day
in the scramble for life
I drop joy scarves
on a bus gone crazy
Let it be me
alone

I clamp my eyelids
in the whirl of a hunt
a troubadour in dust haze
I am cocooned in a haze
Let it be me
alone

When weary from hunting
I drop on the earth
Harsh paper wipes the beads
of my aspirations
Let it be me
alone

at the junction of farewells
unanswered letters, hugs cut
with the precision of thunder
and if it be me
alone

outside of the hearth
with my great coats
there shall be no chattering teeth

TRIAL

The invitation came in gold
Come bask on
a splashing beach
salt is awash
to sweeten horizons.
Racing, I came
with joy, like the joy of a fig tree
barren, suddenly bearing legionfold

I would sift pink shells
mould aesthetic icons, moments eternal
I sparkled, prospecting
a sliver of sun,
the approval of waters when
I carve my initials in sand

Truly, I danced
at the turtle's toe-mark
An octopus tale bore
big idea for a short story

Until you flung my
purple hat on sand
till you decreed
aridity in pink shells

Crushing, making to sound
what second ticks your pulse
a crabbyjingle on hollow paint can
is the finding of my research

A weakening sun flings
javelins of warm gold
on my sunglasses, a gold
card lies shredded

Dashed shells, thrashed hat
I read nostalgic lines,
Tremendous sentences are born
when ocean and man stand trial.

IMPACT

I am all a stammering
dead quiet
before your tenderness

O Word, O God!

A REJOICING

A crazy storm
stampedes the arctic silence
it would batter the straightened shelves
with winds screaming 'Come O Come'

Seven trumpets herald the traffic
wardens guarding the passageways
of discordant jazz
They stop at the first valley in memoriam
They greet life with trembling and faith
gardeners of dream, evergreen trees, peculiar people
silence would buy them a bribe
but their proud fire burns fiercely
their eyes drum, they are scented longings,
iron heat, so sunny they burn our eyes,
textured wall, of torn safety nets.

Stoked coals, pulsating...
I seek candled corridors
to arrive at the sturdy bridge
Empower me to cross over.

Second look...

YOU SAY YOUR MOUTH HAS NO BLOOD

You say your mouth has no blood?
Three times I touched it
three times I touched blood
three times clotting and fresh

Who ate the
head in the freezer
the liver in the cooler
who stole in a heaving car?

See murdered dreams, your legacy,
how many pints swamp your blood bank
O cohort of vultures?

A THAWING

After the womb weeps her red blood
she arches towards him
a plant is slowly, slowly threading its way to light
he runs, she swims beneath his feet
glimpses of secrets file past
in the hot shop of bodytalk
memory trains her telescope on him
Once he was magnificent
he is now diminished in the eye of her
sunglasses
he is still running
see his ears flapping in the wind

Run baby run
dive into a nail bed.

STREAMS I

Where dragonflies feed
Where clouds query the sun
Streams splash in your eyes
in the unravelling lines
Of convoluted buses
Dear woman brimming with whys
searching the venom of police guns
The yawning graves of our pathways
May corn cobs salute your teeth.

STREAMS II

The earth is mud under your high heels
You would release a torrent of jasmine
and pray for open heavens
Your ache is a circumcised penis
ebony streaks of charcoal
champion wrestler of big boys
Your lips are yet dawn
do not suck on blood
Be my gold earrings
let me brush you in warm soap
let me rinse you in spring water.

STREAMS III

Because you love
You know the hibiscus can sprout thorns
in battles older than fire
You carve new tables
coaxing the wayfarers to rice and true dreams,
breasting the narrow path in male pants...
And at the hour when laurels are won,
you toast your womanity with tears
in a shower of black soap
giving the wind a wild grip on your hair.

AN EYE IS TALKING

(On October 1)

MORNING

At the junction
On jack-roads
We invoked the green banners of the earth
The potential of doves
We excavated dreams
Oceans became true Jacuzzis
We toasted a gallery of kisses
With the flaring citation of fireworks.

EVENING

Our kisses are freeze-framed
We slip on banana traps
engineered by cold facts
jigsaw puzzles are turning aside
Criss-crossing the house of aborted oil

Hey, who is the dry-cleaner of this hour.

NIGHT

Behold the scowls that decrease our face value
This is the night
Welcome to the vigil of septic pits
This is the storm
This, the solid sheet of shattered eggs
Where is the dry-cleaner of this hour?

Shouldn't we confess our snores at Gethsemane
confess our common scrawl
how we laughed at our shackled feet
the sword in our hearts
the shroud, consort for three days

DAY

If we would slash headlines, pay offs, body copies
if blood would be a canopy over us, diesel inside us
faggots bearing the onus of solid flames...
let fires raise the anthems of homecoming.

NAKED TESTIMONIES 1

I tell a tale of sour tangerines
and shrivelled penises
in the furnace of testicle crushers
diamonds are mere stones
in the trauma of dry sentences
Tornados chase poetry
And wedding rings and half circles

Where is the voice of my teacher?

NAKED TESTIMONIES II

I embrace myself
in the bowels of my foremothers
discarding second-hand kisses
I see hearths crumble
in courtyards of ruin
absurd altars say I am sacrifice
taverns inflict their wounds
in a reign of swastikas
hasten the night songs.

Who will raise my dead?

NAKED TESTIMONIES III

Still Russian winter, rise to hug me
before the swinging axe
My brass shields are tarnished
Skirts and sweet potatoes suffer loss
Searchlights unearth a judgement of stones
The wedding album is a funeral
time, a penetrable eyeball
anger walks barefoot
in the fury of fallen stars
a lighthouse goes bonkers

Do not be a hut in a melon field

NAKED TESTIMONIES IV

Lies rage in this land
betrayals bewilder time
It is the hour of aluminium fingers
the unreachable itch
bereaved of bathroom slippers
Our limbs are mush-dipped
Muck rules our rivers
Our eyes snap open
before rude toll-gates
At the crossroads,
centrifugal winds caress each hour.

NAKED TESTIMONIES V

The candle burns
without razzmatazz
flames arouse the valleys
a shovel restores the walls
a voice is against the bull
like a mighty man
Pines are springing up in the wasteland
It is I
striding upon my high places
Shield my voice
I walk in fire.

Affirmation...

LADEN

Upon poetry
shall we meet
romping in baths of metaphor
images will ignite our eyes
balls, fires, neons of word shall we be

Let this appointment
be sealed in diaries

As we met in a harried hour
over a desk, some tables
silence,
word was leaden
was pus
But we shall lance
the boil with vaseline
And talk!

RAIN

Say to us
Desolation shall no longer marry this land
every ruler-thief shall be
burned as fuel for the fire
my vow shall entwine its roots deep in truth
and bear a sheltering nest, your great reward
you'll dare again to ensure the eggs of hope
trusting the chicks shall not be scrap metal

Say to us
I shall weave blankets and fashion crutches
that the crippled may walk
I shall marshal joy in a hundred diverse ways
against the insistent sorrow of these bitter years
I shall rule with laughter devoid of guile
for love shall be a signet ring
upon my right hand.

Say
Red graffiti shall no longer war on city walls
just call me, call me in Vesuvius
In the ripple of laughter, call me
Call me empathy, pine music
fresh grain, feeling flesh
I am rain come to ravage the drought.

SIDEWALK LULLABY

Helpless, you see dimly as behind a dark glass
You are thinking of beachsand battered with salt tears
You whimper to the heavens
from swaddling clothes and a hornet's nest

I am quietening you, darling
You will still be honoured
and expel the cold sidewalk, cold life bins
the swirling riverbank flooded to kiss
you with death.
The crescent moon will wear a wide
grin on the face of your night and
you will hear the sound of many laughters
like the sound of many parents or frying fish

Your bruises will be trained advocates staking
legal claims to being no battle field
you will eat bread from my hands.

YOU CANNOT AVOID ME

I am your allowance
at the assembly
the state of your house
the whores at brothels
all shouts you invest on self
you drink my blood,
everyday, I am that crystal.

I am your knife,
your spoon, your fork
though I never taste
the fare of chefs

I, your peak cap
your rulers beads
gold decking your hands
how can you dodge me?

I bear the gourmet choice
to your rare car
my sweat tarred the tarmac
for your sirened presence

Of course, definitive statements
are made when
I barrow your rust
to the dumps

I, your nightmare
stain on different whites
whether we meet or not,
you cannot avoid me!

UNTITLED

When hope flutters like a tremulous candle
like a quaking foundation
when hope is all a flutter on a
faith supporting machine
In that precarious time
I know the astounding calm in the
eye of a storrn
I know the morning star and its full vow
In the light of your birth
So when you become my drink of hyssop
when manna is bitter flavoured
I will hold your sure word
knowing it is spirit and blood

FRESH DAWNS

There are lacerations
but we shall salve our wounds
calm sandstorms, quiet this cyclone
that is a tornado about us,
we shall open fresh log books

And let our feet sing
so far have we trekked on the trail of light
searching for proofs and proud events,
soaring and proud like an eagle in flight.

www.ingramcontent.com/pod-product-compliance
Lightning Source LLC
Chambersburg PA
CBHW020019050426
42450CB00005B/552